CW01019554

THE FINGER
poems 1966-1969

By the same author

THE ISLAND a novel

THE GOLD DIGGERS short stories

POEMS 1950 – 1965

THE FINGER
poems 1966-1969

ROBERT CREELEY

CALDER & BOYARS · LONDON

First published in Great Britain 1970
by Calder and Boyars Ltd
18 Brewer Street London W1

ISBN 0 7145 0422 X Cloth edition
ISBN 0 7145 0423 8 Paper edition

A specially bound and limited edition of one hundred copies has been numbered and signed by the author and is available hors commerce from the publishers.

Grateful acknowledgement is made to the following publications in which some of these poems first appeared: Anonym; Artists and Writers Protest; Best & Co.; Choice; The English Record; Espejo; Evergreen Review; Hierophant; The Lampeter Muse; Lillabulero; Minnesota Review; Mother; Mundus Artium; New Mexico Quarterly; Noose; A Nosegay in Black; Paris Review; Partisan Review; Poetry; Presence; Quixote; The Spectrum; Stony Brook; and Tusitalia.

Acknowledgement is also made to the Black Sparrow Press for the poems used in *Pieces* (in collaboration with Bobbie Creeley) and *The Finger* (an earlier publication of the title poem in collaboration with Bobbie Creeley) copyright 1968 Robert Creeley; to the Brownstone Press for its use of "Gemini" in its publication *The Zodiac*; to Edition Domberger for its use of "Numbers" in its publication *Numbers* (in collaboration with Robert Indiana); to the Gallery Upstairs for its poster publication of "The Boy"; to the Goliard Press for its publication of "A Sight" (in collaboration with R. B. Kitaj); to William Katz for his use of "Kate's" in his publication *Stamped Indelibly*; to the Perishable Press for its broadside publication of "For Joel"; and to the Poets Press for the poems used in its publication *5 Numbers*.

Finally I should like to thank The Rockefeller Foundation for a grant in writing, which was of significant help to me.

Printed in Great Britain by
Clarke, Doble & Brendon Ltd., Plymouth

for Bobbie

Contents

A*

Things continue, but my sense is that I have, at best, simply taken place with that fact. I see no progress in time or any other such situation. So it is that what I feel, in the world, is the one thing I know myself to be, for that instant. I will never know myself otherwise.

Intentions are the variability of all these feelings, moments of that possibility. How can I ever assume that they must come to this or that substance? I am trying to say that what I think to say is of no help to me—and yet insist on my seriousness, which is a sense of my nature I would like to admire.

Words will not say anything more than they do, and my various purposes will not understand them more than what they say.

R. C.

THE HOLE 1

THEY

I wondered what had
happened to the chords.
There was a music,

they were following
a pattern. It was
an intention perhaps.

No field
but they walk
in it. No place

without them, any
discretion is useless.
They want a time, they

have a time, each
one in his place, an
endless arrival.

A METHOD

Patterns
of sounds, endless
discretions, whole
pauses of nouns,

clusters. This
and that, that
one, this
and that. Looking,

seeing, some
thing, being
some. A piece

15

of cake upon,
a face, a fact, that
description like
as if then.

A SIGHT

Quicker
than that, can't
get off "the
dead center of"

myself. *He/I*
were walking. Then
the place *is/was*
not ever enough. But

the house, if
admitted, were
a curiously wrought
complexity of flesh.

The eyes
windows, the head
roof form with
stubbornly placed

bricks of chimney.
I can remember, I
can. Then when
she first touched me,

when we were
lying in that bed,
was the feeling of
falling into no

16

matter we both lay
quiet, where
was it. I
felt her flesh

enclose mine. *Cock*,
they say, *prick*, *dick*,
I put it in her,
I lay there.

Come back, breasts,
come. Back. The sudden
thing of being
no one. I

never felt guilty,
I was confused but
could not feel
wrong, about it.

I wanted to kill her.
I tried it, tentatively,
just a little
hurt. Hurt me.

So immense she was.
All the day
lying flat, lying it seemed
upon a salty sea, the houses

bobbing
around her, under
her, I hung on
for dear life to her.

But when
now I walk, when
the day comes
to trees and a road,

where
is she. Oh, on my
hands and knees, crawl-
ing forward.

PIECES

I didn't
want
to hurt you.
Don't

stop
to think. It
hurts,
to live

like this,
meat
sliced
walking.

THE CIRCLE

Houses in
the ring
to pass through,
past the

accumulated
sense of them,
I know
everyone.

18

I am
stumbling, my
feet are
awkwardly placed.

The man
who says
hello to me
is another

man, another
comes then. One
by one
the women who

look
after. In-
side the
thinking.

THE HOLE

There is
a silence
to fill. A
foot, a fit,

fall,
filled. If
you are
not careful all

the water spills.
One day
at the lake I took
off my bathing
suit

19

in the water,
peed
with pleasure, all
out, all

the water. Wipe
yourself, into
the tight
ass paper is pushed. Fatty

Arbuckle, the one
hero of the school,
took a coke bottle,
pushed it up his girl.

But I
wouldn't dare,
later,
felt there,

opened
myself.
Broken glass,
broken silence,

filled with screaming,
on the bed
she didn't want
it, but said, after,

the only time
it felt right. Was
I to force
her. Mother,

sister, once
seen, had breasts.
My father
I can't remember

but a man
in some building,
we were all swimming,
took out his

to piss, it
was large. He was
the teacher.
Everywhere

there is pleasure,
deep,
with hands
and feet.

I want
to, now I
can't wait any
longer. Talk

to me, fill
emptiness with
you, empty
hole.

A PRAYER

Bless
something small
but infinite
and quiet.

There are senses
make an object
in their simple
feeling for one.

THE FLOWER

Remember the way you
hunched up the first
times in bed, all your
body as you walked

seemed centered
in your breasts. It
was watching the world
come toward me, I felt

so alive and honoured.
Me—least of all possibilities,
yet in bed before you,
the patient flower.

SAME

Why am I
the laggard, as if
broken charms
were debris only.

Some thought
of it, broken
watch spring—
is not rusted merely.

That is all
they talk of
in Madrid, as much
to say the same.

The same thing
said the same
place is
the same.

Left in pieces,
objectively—
putting it
back together.

THERE

A place so
hostile it does

not want
any more, not

even not wanting,
is there.

Would one walk
or run, or avoid,

whatever—at
that moment

a voice
so tense

trying to
be acknowledged.

JOY

I could look at
an empty hole for hours
thinking it will
get something in it,

will collect
things. There is
an infinite emptiness
placed there.

A PICTURE

A little
house with
small
windows,

a gentle
fall of the
ground to
a small

stream. The trees
are both close
and green, a tall
sense of enclosure.

There is a sky
of blue
and a faint sun
through clouds.

A PIECE

One and
one, two,
three.

THE BOX
for John Chamberlain

Three sides,
four
windows. Four

doors, three
hands.

WATER MUSIC

The words are a beautiful music.
The words bounce like in water.

Water music,
loud in the clearing

off the boats,
birds, leaves.

They look for a place
to sit and eat—

no meaning,
no point.

THEY (2)

They were trying to catch up.
But from the distance

between them, one thought
it would be a long time

even with persistent
running. They were walking

slower and slower
for hours and hours.

WAS

The face
was
beautiful.

25

She was
a pleasure.
She

tried
to please.

THE FARM

Tips of celery,
clouds of

grass—one
day I'll go away.

INDIANS

Big, wise
man. The happy
woman

in a place
she found. He
waited

in the clearing.

ENOUGH

1

It is possible, in words, to speak
of what has happened—a sense

of there and here, now
and then. It is some other

26

way of being, prized enough,
that it makes a common

ground. Once
you were

alone and I
met you. It was late

at night.
I never

left after that,
not to my own mind,

but stayed
and stayed. Years

went by. What
were they. Days—

some happy
but some bitter

and sad. If I walked
across the room, then,

and saw you un-
expected, saw the particular

whiteness of
your body, a little

older, more
tired—in words

I possessed it, in
my mind I thought, and

you never knew
it, there I danced

for you, stumbling, in
the corner of my eye.

2

Don't we dance
a little bit,

slowly,
slowly. My

legs
will work

to the tunes of
a happy time.

3

A distance
separates, ob-

jectively, as from
shore, water, an

island projected,
up, against

the sun, a smoke
haze, drifting,

reflects
the golden city

now. Your
head and hands,

your eyes once
in words were

lakes but
this is an ocean

of vagueness. The sun
goes out. I

try to feel
where you are.

4

Hoo, hoo—
laughter.

Hoo, hoo—
laughter.

Obscene
distance. The

mind makes
its own

forms, looks
into its terror

so
selfishly

alone. Such
a fact so simply

managed there is
no need for any

one else. All
by myself I see

the obscene bodies
twisting, twisting,

my hand
explores their

delight, un-
noticed, my body

shrinks
back.

5

One
by one
the form

comes. One
thing follows
another. One

and one,
and one. Make
a picture

for the world
to be. It
will be.

6

You
there, me

here, or is it
me

there, you
here—there

or there
or here—and here.

In two
places, in two

pieces
I think.

7

Your body is a garbage can.
Your body is white, why

let others touch it, why
not. Why

my body so
tentative, do I

like the pain
of such impossible understanding.

Your body
is a white

softness, it has
its own

place time
after time.

8

I vow to my life to respect it.
I will not wreck it.

I vow to yours to be
enough, enough, enough.

HERE

What
has happened
makes

the world.
Live
on the edge,

looking.

31

INTERVALS

Who
am I—
identity
singing.

Place
a lake
on ground, water
finds a form.

Smoke
on the air
goes higher
to fade.

Sun bright,
trees dark green,
a little movement
in the leaves.

Birds singing
measure distance,
intervals between
echo silence.

WATER

Water drips,
a fissure of leaking
moisture spills
itself unnoticed.

What
was I looking at,
not to see
that wetness spread.

THE EYE

The eye I look out of
or hands I use,
feet walking,
they stay particular.

I wanted
one place to be
where I was
always.

I wanted you
somehow equal,
my love, one says—
I speak with that body.

But then it happens—
another time, a particular
circumstance—surrounded by such
a distance.

You took my heart
which was with you,
you took my hands
which I used for you.

Oh when regrets stop
and the silence comes
back to be
a place still for us,

our bodies will tell
their own story, past
all error,
come back to us.

OF YEARS

Of a few years
come into focus—
peace and understanding,
the uneasy virtues.

Of a mist.
A night's peace
waking to sullenness,
uneasy companion—

of force,
of coercion, compulsion,
of nagging, insistent
suspicion.

Of nothing
more than a moment.
Sudden candle light
shattered the night.

SONG

How simply
        for another
pace the virtues,
        peace and goodwill.

Sing pleasure,
        the window's opening,
unseen back of it
        the door closes.

How peace, how happiness,
        locked as insistence,
force weather, see sun,
        and won't look back.

34

FOR JOEL

Some simple
virtue of silence
you taught me once,
not to talk too much.

In your place, waiting,
up all night, talking
and drinking, flowers
for your wife then—

but not accepted.
The test was
how much unhappiness
either one of us could endure.

I think of friends,
some known for years.
There are men
made sense for me.

Measures—
ways of being in one's life,
happy or unhappy,
never dead to it.

Joy to the marriage, now,
of such a friend
gave me such reassurance
in his own pain,

joy to strength and weakness,
to what won't go dead
to its own pleasure
but likes to laugh.

A full shout
for happiness, a
bride of such delight,
a groom so wise.

A BIRTHDAY

Shall we address it
as you, lovely one,
singing those intervals

of a complex
loneliness, a wanting too
to know

its condition. Together
is one by one,
and a beauty

comes of it, a substance
of beauty—beauty, *beauty*—
dripping its condition.

I had thought
a moment of stasis
possible, some

thing fixed—
days, worlds—
but what I know

is water, as you
are water, as you
taught me water

is wet. Now slowly
spaces occur, a ground is
disclosed as dirt. The

mountains come of it,
the sky precedes, and where
there had been only

land now sticks and stones
are evident. So we are
here, so we are.

36

DANCING

To be dancer
of my own dismay,
to let my legs and arms
move in their own feeling,

I make a form of assumptions
as real as clothes on a line,
a car moving
that sees another coming,

dancing as all would
were it not for what it thought
it was always doing,
or could leave

itself to itself
whatever it is, dancing,
or better, a jerking leap
toward impulse.

A TALLY

A tally of forces, consequent
memories, of times and places—
habits of preparation at other
points of time and place.

And the hand found the fingers
still on it, moved the thumb,
easily, to the forefinger,
still worked. What

has come. Age? But,
to know itself, needs
occasion, as, no longer young
wants a measure.

The mirror the mind is,
reflective, in that guise,
long habit of much delaying thought
to savor terms of the impression—

it's not as bad as one thought,
but that is relative. Not as simple
as the boat is leaking, he, she, it,
they—or we, you and I, are sinking.

Within the world, this one, many quirks
accomplished, effected, in the thought,
I don't know how, I only live here,
with the body I walk in.

Hence I love you, I did, do,
a moment ago it was daylight,
now dark I wonder what the memory means,
loving you more than I had thought to.

No agreement to stay, see it out,
the dereliction of fleshy duties—
but not burn down the house
for whatever rage was once.

"OH MY LOVE . . ."

Oh my love,
in other times
the things we are
were beauty too.

In ways that were
I never knew
were possible
might talk to you.

38

Or on and on
and up and down
seasons and days
might make a place

unlike such
awkwardness makes
this one awkward
fall apart.

FRAGMENTS

Decorous, and forbearing further correction,
to the empty halls he announces
pardon. No wound deeper than
death, he says, not knowing.

_____

The fall of
feet dancing
to sounds within
his hearing. Oh,
how much he heard.

_____

Little song, sing
days of happiness. Make
a pardonable wonder
of one's blunders.

PIECES 2

for Louis Zukofsky

As real as thinking
wonders created
by the possibility—

forms. A period
at the end of a sentence
which

began *it was*
into a present,
a presence

saying
something
as it goes.

                .

No forms less
than activity

All words—
days—or
eyes—

or happening
is an event only
for the observer?

No one
there. Everyone
here.

                .

Small facts
of eyes, hair
blonde, face

43

looking like a
flat painted
board. How

opaque as if
a reflection
merely, skin

vague glove of
randomly seen
colours.

.

Inside
and out

impossible
locations—

reaching in
from out-

side, out
from in-

side—as
middle:

one
hand.

.   .   .

FLOWERS

> No knowledge rightly understood
> can deprive us of the mirth of flowers.
> —Edward Dahlberg

No thing less than one thing
or more—

no sun
but sun—

or water
but wetness found—

What truth is it
that makes men so miserable?

Days we die
are particular—

This life cannot be lived
apart from what it must forgive.

. . .

THE FAMILY

Father
and mother
and sister
and sister
and sister.

.

Here we are.
There are five
ways to say this.

. . .

KATE'S

If I were you
and you were me
I bet you'd
do it too.

. . .

45

FOR YOU

Like watching rings extend in water
this time of life.

.   .   .

A STEP

Things
        come and go.
Then
        let them.

.   .   .

Having to—
what do I think
to say now.

Nothing but
comes and goes
in a moment.

.

Cup.
Bowl.
Saucer.
Full.

.

The way into the form,
the way out of the room—

The door, the hat,
the chair, the fact.

.

Sitting, waves on the beach,
or else clouds, in the sky,

a road, going by,
cars, a truck, animals, in crowds.

.   .   .

The car
moving
the hill
down

which yellow
leaves
light forms
declare.

.

Car coughing moves with
a jerked energy forward.

.

Sit. Eat
a doughnut.

Love's consistency
favours me.

.

A big crow on the
top of the tree's
form more stripped
with leaves gone
overweights it.

.   .   .

Pieces of cake crumbling
in the hand trying to hold
them together to give each
of the seated guests a piece.

.

Willow, the house, an egg—
what do they make?

Hat, happy, a door—
what more.

.   .   .

THE FINGER

Either in or out of
the mind, a conception
overrides it. *So that*
that time I was a stranger,

bearded, with clothes that were
old and torn. I was told,
it was known to me, my
fate would be timeless. Again

and again I was to
get it right, the story I
myself knew only the way of,
but the purpose if it

had one, was not mine.
The quiet shatter of the light,
the image folded into
endlessly opening patterns—

had they faced me into
the light so that my

48

eye was blinded? At moments
I knew they had gone but

searched for her face, the pureness
of its beauty, the endlessly sensual—
but no sense as that now reports it.
Rather, she was beauty, that

Aphrodite I had known of,
and caught sight of as *maid*—
a girlish openness—or known
as a woman turned from the light.

I knew, however, the other,
perhaps even more. She was there
in the room's corner, as she would be,
bent by a wind it seemed

would never stop blowing,
braced like a seabird,
with those endlessly clear grey eyes.
Name her, Athena—what name.

The osprey, the sea, the waves.
To go on telling the story,
to go on though no one hears it,
to the end of my days?

Mercury, Hermes, in dark glasses.
Talk to him—but as if
one talked to the telephone,
telling it to please listen—

is that right, have I said it—
and the reflecting face echoes
some cast of words in mind's eye,
attention a whip of surmise.

And the power to tell
is glory. One unto one

unto one. And though all
mistake it, it is one.

I saw the stones thrown
at her. I felt a radiance transform
my hands and my face.
I blessed her, I was one.

Are there other times?
Is she that woman,
or this one. Am I the man—
and what transforms.

Sit by the fire.
I'll dance a jig I learned
long before we were born
for you and you only then.

I was not to go
as if to somewhere,
was not in the mind
as thinking knows it,

but danced in a jigging
intensive circle
before the fire and its heat
and that woman lounging.

How had she turned herself?
She was largely warm—
flesh heavy—and smiled
in some deepening knowledge.

There are charms.
The pedlar and the small dog
following and the whistled,
insistent song.

I had the pack,
the tattered clothing,

was neither a man nor not one,
all that—

and who was she,
with the fire behind her,
in the mess of that place,
the dust, the scattered pieces,

her skin so warm,
so massive, so stolid in her
smiling the charm did not
move her but rather

kept her half-sleepy attention,
yawning, indulging the manny
who jiggled a world before her
made of his mind.

She was young,
she was old,
she was small.
She was tall with

extraordinary grace. Her face
was all distance, her eyes
the depth of all one had thought of,
again and again and again.

To approach, to hold her,
was not possible.
She laughed and turned
and the heavy folds of cloth

parted. The nakedness
burned. Her heavy breath,
her ugliness, her lust—
but her laughing, her low

chuckling laugh, the way
she moved her hand to the

naked breast, then to
her belly, her hand with its fingers.

Then *shone*—
and whatever is said
in the world, or forgotten,
or not said, makes a form.

The choice is simply,
I will—as mind is a finger,
pointing, as wonder
a place to be.

Listen to me, let
me touch you
there. You are young again,
and you are looking at me.

Was there ever
such foolishness more
than what thinks it knows
and cannot see, was there ever

more? Was the truth
behind us, or before?
Was it one
or two, and who was I?

She was laughing, she was
laughing, at me,
and I danced, and
I danced.

Lovely, lovely woman, let
me sing, *one to
one to one*, and let
me follow.

.　.　.

One thing
done, the
rest follows.

    .

Not from not
but in in.

    .

Here here
here. Here.

  .   .   .

I cannot see you
there for what you
thought you were.

The faded memories
myself enclose
passing too.

    .

Were you there
or here now—
such a slight sound
what was your step makes.

    .

Here I
am. There
you are.

    .

53

The head
of a
pin on . . .

.

Again
and again
now
also.

.   .   .

GEMINI

Two eyes, two hands—
in one two are given.

The words
are messages

from another,
not understood but given.

.

Neither one, nor the other,
nor of a brother—but in

the one, two, restless,
confined to a place ruled

by a moon, and another one
with messages, rather, sequences

of words that are not to be understood
but somehow given to a world.

All this dances in a room,
two by two, but alone.

.

From one to two,
is the first rule.

Of two minds the twin
is to double life given.

.

What it says is that one
is two, the twin,

that the messenger comes
to either, that these fight

to possess, but do not
understand——that if the

moon rules, there is
"domestic harmony"——but if the blood

cry, the split so divide,
there can be no

company for the two in one.
He is alone.

.   .   .

In secret
the out's in——

the wise
surprised, all

going coming,
begun undone.

Hence the fool dances
in endless happiness.

.

A circling with
snake-tail in mouth—

what the head was
looked *forward*,

what backward is,
then guess.

Either way,
it will stay.

. . .

"Time" is some sort of hindsight, or else rhythm of
activity—e.g., now it's 11 days later—"also alive" like
they say.

.

Where it is
was and
will be never
only here.

.

—fluttering as
  falling, leaves,
  knives, to
  avoid—tunnel
  down the
  vague sides . . .

.

—it
  it—

. . .

"FOLLOW THE DRINKING GOURD . . ."

Present again
present present
again present
present again

leaves falling,
knives, a windspout
of nostalgic faces,
into the air.

Car glides forward.
Drive from Bloomington,
Indiana to Lexington,
Ky. Here the walls

of fall, the stone,
the hill, the trucks
in front with
the unseen drivers.

Stoney Lonesome. Gnaw—
bone. A house
sits back from
the road.

A Christmas
present—all
present and ac-
counted for? Sir?

Passage of time.
The sun shone level
from the left-
hand side of

the land—a flat-
seeming distance,
left, east? South?
Sun shines.

Go on. Tell
me, them, him,
her, their
apparent forms.

The "present dented",
call it "long
distance", come
here home. Then

a scarecrow there, here a
snowman. Where in
the world then an-
other place?

Drive on
what seems an
exceptionally smooth
and even surface,

the forward cars
way up there glint
in that sun of
a universe of mine.

And for twenty eight
dollars—all this.
All in the mind
in time in place—

what it costs to rent
agency? Give
me a present, your
hand to help

me understand this.
So far, so long,
so anywhere a
place if not this

one—driving,
screaming a lovely
song perhaps, or
a cigar smoke—

"When they were
young in Kentucky
a man to freedom
took them in a cave . . ."

A famous song,
to drive to,
sing along the
passing way—

or *done* or
right or
wrong or
wander on.

.   .   .

THE MOON

Earlier in the evening the moon
was clear to the east,
over the snow of the yard
and fields—a lovely

bright clarity and perfect
roundness, isolate,
riding as they say the
black sky. Then we went

about our businesses of the
evening, eating supper, talking,
watching television, then
going to bed, making love,

and then to sleep. But before
we did I asked her to look

59

out the window at the moon
now straight up, so that

she bent her head and looked
sharply up, to see it.
Through the night it must
have shone on, in that

fact of things—another
moon, another night—a
full moon in the winter's
space, a white loneliness.

I came awake to the blue
white light in the darkness,
and felt as if someone
were there, waiting, alone.

.   .   .

NUMBERS

For Robert Indiana

One

What
singular upright flourishing
condition . . .
it enters here,
it returns here.

.

Who was I that
thought it was
another one by
itself divided or multiplied
produces one.

.

This time, this
place, this
one.

.

You are not
me, nor I you.

.

All ways.

.

As of a stick,
stone, some-

thing so
fixed it has

a head, walks,
talks, leads

a life.

.

Two

When they were
first made, all the
earth must have
been their reflected
bodies, for a moment—
a flood of seeming
bent for a moment back
to the water's glimmering—
how lovely they came.

.

What you wanted
I felt, or felt I felt.
This was more than one.

.

This point of so-called
consciousness is forever
a word making up
this world of more
or less than it is.

.

Don't leave me.
Love me. One by one.

.

As if to sit
by me were another
who did sit. So

to make you
mine, in the mind,
to know you.

.

Three

They come now with
one in the middle—
either side thus
another. Do they

know who each other
is or simply walk

with this pivot between them.
Here forms have possibility.

.

When either this
or that becomes
choice, this fact

of things enters.
What had been
agreed now

alters to
two and one,
all ways.

.

The first
triangle, of form,
of people,

sounded a
lonely occasion I
think——the

circle begins
here, intangible—
yet a birth.

.

Four

This number for me
is comfort, a secure
fact of things. The

table stands on
all fours. The dog
walks comfortably,

and two by two
is not an army
but friends who love

one another. Four
is a square,
or peaceful circle,

celebrating return,
reunion,
love's triumph.

.

The card which is the
four of hearts must
mean enduring experience
of life. What other
meaning could it have.

.

Is a door
four—but
who enters.

.

Abstract—yes, as
two and two
things, four things—
one and three.

.

Five

Two by
two with
now another

in the middle
or else at
the side.

    .

From each
of the four
corners draw

a line to
the alternate
points. Where

these intersect
will be
five.

    .

When younger this was
a number used to
count with, and

to imagine a useful
group. Somehow the extra
one—what is more than four—

reassured me there would be
enough. Twos and threes or
one and four is plenty.

    .

A way to draw stars.

.

Six

Twisting
    as forms of it
two and three—

    on the sixth
day had finished
    all creation—

hence holy—
    or that the sun
is "furthest from

    equator & appears
to pause, before
    returning . . ."

or that it "contains
    the first even number
(2) , and the first odd

    number (3) , the former representing
the male member, and the latter
    the *muliebris pudenda* . . ."

Or two triangles interlocked.

.

Seven

We are seven, echoes in
my head like a nightmare of
responsibility—seven
days in the week, seven

years for the itch of
unequivocal involvement.

.

Look
at
the
light
of
this
hour.

.

I was born at seven in
the morning and my
father had a monument
of stone, a pillar, put
at the entrance of the
hospital, of which he was head.

.

*At sixes
and sevens*—the pen
lost, the paper:

a night's dead
drunkenness. Why
the death of something now

so near if *this*
number is holy.
Are all

67

numbers one?
Is counting forever
beginning again.

.

Let this be the end of the seven.

.

Eight
──

Say "eight"—
be patient.

Two fours
show the way.

.

Only this number
marks the cycle—

the eight year interval—
for that confluence

makes the full moon shine
on the longest

or shortest
day of the year.

.

Now summer fades.
August its month—
this interval.

.

She is eight
years old, holds
a kitten, and
looks out at me.

.

Where are you.
One table.
One chair.

.

In light lines count the interval.
Eight makes the time wait quietly.

.

No going back—
though half is
four and
half again
is two.

.

Oct-
ag-
on-
al.

.

Nine

There is no point
of rest here.
It wavers,

it reflects multiply
the *three*
times three.

Like a mirror
it returns here
by being there.

.

Perhaps in the
emphasis implicit—
over and over—

"triad of triads",
"triply sacred and perfect
number"—that

resolves what—
in the shifting,
fading containment?

.

Somehow the game
where a nutshell covers
the one object, a

stone or coin, and
the hand is
quicker than the eye—

how is that *nine*,
and not *three*
chances, except that

three imaginations of it
might be, and there are
two who play—

70

making six, but
the world is real also,
in itself.

                .

More. The nine months
of waiting that discover
life or death—

another life or death—
not yours, not
mine, as we watch.

                .

The serial diminish-
ment or progression of
the products which

helped me remember:
nine times two is one-eight
                [*nine times nine is eight-one*—
at each end,

move forward, backward,
then, and the same
numbers will occur.

                .

What law
or
mystery

is involved
protects
itself.

                .

71

Zero

Where are you—who
    by not being here
are here, but here
    by not being here?

There is no trick to reality—
    a mind
makes it, any
    mind. You

walk the years in a
    nothing, a no
place I know as well as
    the last breath

I took, blowing the smoke
    out of a mouth
will also go nowhere,
    having found its way.

.

Reading that primitive systems
seem to have natural cause for
the return to one, after ten—
but this is *not* ten—out of
nothing, one, to return to that—
Americans have a funny way—
somebody wrote a poem about it—
of "doing nothing"—What else
should, *can*, they do?

.

What
by being not

72

is—is not
by being.

.

When holes taste good
we'll put them in our bread

.

The Fool

"With light step, as if earth and its trammels had little
power to restrain him, a young man in gorgeous vestments
pauses at the brink of a precipice among the great heights
of the world; he surveys the blue distance before him—its
expanse of sky rather than the prospect below. His act of
eager walking is still indicated, though he is stationary
at the given moment; his dog is still bounding. The edge
which opens on the depth has no terror; it is as if angels
were waiting to uphold him, if it came about that he leaped
from the height. His countenance is full of intelligence and
expectant dream. He has a rose in one hand and in the
other a costly wand, from which depends over his right
shoulder a wallet curiously embroidered. He is a prince of
the other world on his travels through this one—all amidst
the morning glory, in the keen air. The sun, which shines
behind him, knows whence he came, whither he is going,
and how he will return by another path after many
days . . ."

. . .

The bedpost is an
extraordinary shape
to have happened though
in nature this upthrust

with its conical cap and
bulging middle is met
with often enough. But the
bar, horizontal, joining

the two posts, I have not
seen this elsewhere except
as the cross bar of the collar
bone, my own, or those of others.

　　　　.

What she says she wants
she wants she says.

　　.　　.　　.

One/the Sun/
Moon/one.

　　　　.

How far one has come
in these seven league boots.

　　　　.

The pen,
the lines it
leaves, forms
divine—nor
laugh nor giggle.
This prescription
is true.
Truth is a scrawl,
all told
in all.

　　　　.

Back where things were
sweeter, water falls
and thinks again.

                .

Here, there,
every-
where.

                .

Never write
to say more
than saying
something.
_____

Words
are
pleasure.
All
words.

                .

NAMES

Harry has written
all he knows.
Miriam tells
her thought, Peter
says again
his mind. Robert and John,
William, Tom,
and Helen, Ethel,
that woman whose name
he can't remember

or she even him
says to tell
all they know.

. . .

Can feel it in the pushing,
not letting myself relax
for any reason, hanging on.

.

Thinking—and coincident
experience of the situation.

"I think he'll hit me."
He does. Etc.

.

Reflector/ -ive/ -ed.

.

CHICAGO

Say that you're
        lonely—and want
something to
        place you—

going around groping
        either by mind
or hand—but behind
        the pun is a

door you keep open,
        one way,

76

so they won't touch you
        and still let you stay.

.

I can't see in
        this place more
than the walls
        and door—
a light flat
        and air hot,
and drab, drab, drab
        and locked.

_____

Would dying be here?
Never go anywhere you
        can't live.

_____

Concrete blocks painted an ''off white'' yellow tone—in-
stitutional—*very* noisy, senses of people next side of wall,
etc. Get *used* to shrinking space—They'll let you out when
there's reason.

. . .

Pleasures of pain,
        oh lady,
fail in the argument—
        This way

of making friends
        you made me let
go of, losing myself
        in a simple fact.

.

NYC—

Streets as ever blocky, grey—square sense of rectangu-
lar enclosures, emphasized by the coldness of the time of
year, and the rain. In moving in the cab—continual sense
of small (as size, i.e., all "cars", etc.) persistent diffi-
culties.

.

THE FRIENDS

I want to help you
by understanding what
you want me to
understand by saying so.

.

I listen. I had
an ego once upon
a time—I do still,
for you listen to me.

Let's be very still.
Do you hear? Hear
what, I will say when-
ever you ask me to listen.

.

I wouldn't joke about
your wife wanting to wash
her hair at eleven o'clock
at night but supposing she

wants to I'd consider her
thoughts on the matter equally

78

with yours wherever you were
and for whatever reason.

.

Don't think I'm
so awful you can
afford my company
so as not to
put me down more.

.

God, I hate
simplistic logic like—
I like it. Who cares.

.

Liking is as
liking does
for you, for me.

.

The "breathtaking banalities"
one only accomplishes in
retrospect. Hindsight—

they call it— like the
backend of a horse. *Horse's
ass*, would be the way.

. . .

DICTION

The grand time when the words
were fit for human allegation,

79

and imagination of small, local
containments, and the lids fit.

What was the wind blew through it,
a veritable bonfire like they say—

and did say in hostile, little voices:
"It's changed, it's not the same!"

.

AMERICA

America, you ode for reality!
Give back the people you took.

Let the sun shine again
on the four corners of the world

you thought of first but do not
own, or keep like a convenience.

People are your own word, you
invented that locus and term.

Here, you said and say, is
where we are. Give back

what we are, these people you made,
us, and nowhere but you to be.

.

CITIZEN

Write a giggly ode about
        motherfuckers—Oedipus—
or Lysergic Acid—a word
        for an experience, verb

or noun. Count down, count
        Orlovsky, count up—

in the air, you filthy
　　　window washer. Why

not clean up the world.
　　　You need it, I
need it—more than
　　　either one of us can get.

　　．

PLACE

Thinking of you asleep on a
　　　bed on a pillow, on a
　　　bed—the ground or space

you lie on. That's enough to
　　　talk to now I got space and
　　　time like a broken watch.

　　．

Hello there—instant
reality on the other
end of this so-called line.

　　．

Oh no you
don't, do you?

　　．

Late, the words, late
the form of them, al-

ready past what they were
fit for, one and two and three.

　　．

81

THE PURITAN ETHOS

Happy the man who loves what
he has and worked for it also.

.

There is a lake of clear water.
There are forms of things despite us.

Pope said, "a little learning",
and, and, and, and—the same.

Why don't you go home and sleep
and come back and talk some more.

.

By location, e.g., where
or here—or what words in
time make of things. *Space*,
they say, and think a several

dimensioned locus. Mr.
Warner came from a small
town in the middle mid-
eastern Atlantic states.

That—in time—displaces
all else might be said of
him, or whatever became
of him in that other space he knew.

.

THE PROVINCE

Trying to get "our men
back" and "our ship
back"—"tactical
nuclear weapons"—dig!

Shee-it. The *world*,
      dad, is where you
live unless you've for-
      gotten it through that

incredible means called
      efficacy *or* understanding
or superior lines of
      or, or something else.

      .

CANADA

"The maple leaf forever"
      "in 1867—"
"inspired the world
      to say—"

      .   .   .

Happy love, this
agreement, coincidence
like crossing streets.

      .

Forms face
facts find.

      .

One cock
pheasant one
hen pheasant
walk along.

      .   .   .

THE BOY

Push yourself in on others
hard enough, they beat you
with sticks and whips——the birth

of love. E.g., affection aroused,
it moves to be close, touch, and
feel the warm livingness of an-

other, any other, sucked, stroked,
the club itself possibly a symbol of
the obvious. My mother had hair,

and when I grew older, so did
I, all over my face, which I wanted
to be there, and grew a beard henceforth.

.   .   .

3 IN 1

for Charlotte

The bird
flies
out the
window. She
flies.

.

The bird flies
out the
window. She
flies.

.

The bird
flies. She
flies.

. . .

THEY

What could
they give me I
hadn't myself
discovered—

The *world*,—that
I'd fallen upon
in some
distracted drunkenness—

Or that the rules
were *wrong*, an
observation they
as well as I
knew now—

They were imagination
also. If they
would be as the
mind could see *them*,

then it all was
true and the
mind followed and
I also.

.

ECHO

Yes but your sweetness
derives drunkenness—

over, and over, not
your face, not your

hand—no you nor
me is real now—

Nothing here now,
nothing there now.

.

In this fact of face and body—looking out—a *kind* of
pleasure. That is, no argument stops me. Not—"yes"—
"no"—gradually? Only involved as openings, sexual also,
seem to be—but is "no" my final way of speaking? E.g.,
a "poet" of such impossibilities "I" makes up?

.   .   .

So tired
it falls
apart.

.   .   .

Why say to them
truth is confounded with opposition,
or that—*or that* what is
were a happiness.

Simple, to be said, a life
is nothing more than itself,
and all the bodies together
are, one by one, the measure.

.

I am finally
what I had to be,
neither more nor less—
become happiness.

. . .

Forms' passage as
water beside the white
upright group of apparently
flat buildings—The river's
bend, seen from the sky—
down, under, with the eye.

.

Allen's saying as we fly out of NYC—the look of the city
underneath us like a cellular growth, "cancer"—so that
senses of men on the earth as an investment of it radiates
a world cancer—Burroughs' "law" finally quite clear.

.

Mississippi much as—pen blots with pressure (?)—the
sky ahead a faint light yellow—like "northern" lights.—
Why the goddamn impatience with that AS—the damn
function of *simile*, always a displacement of what *is*
happening.

.

Life like you
think you have
it till it isn't
—but is, inevitably—
behind the scene.

. . .

Days later——neither having
become nor not become a
convenience to assumptions.

.

You look up the street to
the far bay and boats
floating in a sunny haze.

Either way, the streets lead
down, from this hill. An
apartment house of tiered

layers sits opposite on
the far corner. We get
into the car and drive off.

.

Nowhere one
goes will
one ever
be away
enough from
wherever
one was.

.

Falling-in windows——
the greenhouse back of
Curleys' house. The
Curleys were so good
to me, their mother
held me on her lap.

.   .   .

No clouds out the window,
flat faint sky of faded blue.
The sun makes spring now,

a renewal possibly of like energy,
something forgotten almost remembered,
echoes in my mind like the grass.

.

Your opaqueness, at moments,
would be the mirror. Your
face closed as a door—

that insists on nothing,
but not to be entered—
wanting simply to be left alone.

I slept, it seemed, the moment
I lay down in the bed, even,
it might have been, impatient

to be out of it, gone away,
to what densities can be there
in a night's sleep, day by day.

But, all in the mind it comes
and goes. My own life is given
me back again, something forgotten.

.

I want to sing.
What makes it
impossible—so

that one lifts
that dead bulk
with such insistent energy?

.

"But now it's come to distances . . ."
—Leonard Cohen

.

Thinking—a tacit, tactile distance between us at this
moment—much as if we had lives in "different worlds"—
which, I suppose, would be the case despite all closeness
otherwise, i.e., almost as if the moment one were "think-
ing", and not literally taking, finding place in something
we both had occasion in, that this fact of things becomes
a separation. I.e., it seems not possible to live the "same"
life, no matter what one wants, wills, or tries to have the
so-called "case".—Like old "romantic" self-query, come
of obvious unrest and frustration.

. . .

ECHO OF

Can't myself
let off this
fiction. "You
don't exist,

baby, you're
dead." Walk
off, on—the
light bulb

overhead, beside,
or, the bed, you
think you laid
on? When, what.

.

THE

The water
waiting far

off to the
east, the
west—the
shores of the world.

.   .   .

Situation of feeling increasingly "apart" from people in
reading—and/or probably the fact of going *into* the read-
ing to find a place in the welter of randomness of people
there—*or* my assumption, in fatigue, that no one's making
it.

.

You are all lovely,
hairy, scarey
people after all.

.

AGAIN

One more day gone,
done, found in
the form of days.

It began, it
ended—was
forward, backward,

slow, fast, a
sun shone, clouds,
high in the air I was

91

for awhile with others,
then came down
on the ground again.

No moon. A room in
a hotel—to begin
again.

.   .   .

The which it
was, form
seen—there
here, re-
peated for/
as/—There
is a "parallel".

.

When and/or if, as,—however, you do "speak" to people,
i.e., as condition of the circumstance (as Latin: "what's
around") a/n "im (in) pression". "I'll *crush* you to
"death"—"flying home".

.

Allen last night—context of *how* include the output of
human function in an experience thereof makes the fact
of it become possibility of pleasure—not fear, not pain.
Everybody *spends* it (the "life" they inhabit) all—hence,
no problem of that kind, except (*large* fact) in imagina-
tion.

.   .   .

92

In the house of
old friend, whose
friend, my

friend, the trouble
with you, who,
he is, there, here,
we were *not*.

   .

The voice of the
echo of time, the
same—"I

know you," no
pain in that, we are
all around what we are.

   .

(Re Bob's film, CUT)

Pictures of the movement.
Pictures of the red-headed
man going down on—

pictures of the red-
haired man on the red-
headed girl on the—

pictures of the flat form
cutting hair off, the long,
the echoic scissors cutting.

   .

—Like problem of depth perception, each movement to
the familiarity (a 20 year "distance") confronts the

time—as—distance of the "real" event, i.e., *now*—but "here", as a habit, is what we are lacking *here*.

. . .

P.S.

Thinking of Olson—"we are
as we find out we are."

. . .

ICE CREAM

Sure,
Herbert—
Take a bite—

The crowd
milling on the brîdge, the
night forms in

the air. So
much has gone
away.

.

Upside
down
forms
faces.

.

Letter to General
Eisenhower from

General
Mount-

batten.
Better

be
right.

Better batter
bigger pancakes.

You Chief
Eat It.

.

Something that hasn't as yet had chance to
wants the possibility of asking

if what might be might be,
if what has to be is otherwise.

.

Oh so cute in your
gorgeous gown you were.

*You were, you were,
you-are-or-you-were-you-were.*

.   .   .

What
do you think it is.
Dogs wandering
the roads.

All I knew or know
began with this—
emptiness
with its incessant movement.

Where was it—
to be younger, older,
if not here,
if not there.

Calling,
calling over the shoulder,
through a mist,
to those fading people.

.

This singleness
you make an evidence
has purpose.

You are not alone,
however one—not
so alone.

Light finds a place
you can see it in
such singleness.

.

There might be
an imaginary
place to be—
there might be.

.

Grey mist forms
out the window,
leaves showing green,
the dark trunks of trees—

96

place beyond?
The eye sees, the
head apparently records
the vision of these eyes.

What have I seen,
now see? There were
times before
I look now.

.

Re C—
Making a form for you
of something, a vehicle
of the head, round
wheel eyes for getting there.

Why do you get up so
restlessly if sitting down is
where I always find you—
after all these years.

You want to fight?
You want a black eye for
your troubles? How be
young and yet to be loved?

Sprightly, you have a
head I do put wheels on,
and two arms and two legs.
You'll travel.

. . .

Like a man committed to searching
out long darkened corridors with doors,
and only the spot of the flashlight to
be a way into and back out, to safety.

.

Peace, brother, to all of it,
in all senses, in all places,
in every way, in all
senses, in all places, in
every way.

.

Here now *you* are—
by what means?
And who to know it?

.

A lady in a dress of velvet,
a girl in a cotton dress,
a woman, walking—
something like that, with hair—

some form you feel or
you said you felt was
like that the times we sat
and you told me what

to look for—this
fact of some woman
with some man like
that was really all.

.

The sun will set again on
the edge of the sky or whatever

you want to call it. *Out there*,
not here, the sun ''will set,

98

did set, is *now* setting".
Hear, goddamnit, hear.

.

I have no ease
calling things beautiful
which are by that
so called to my mind.

.

You want
the fact
of things
in words,
of words.

.

Endless trouble, endless pleasure,
endless distance, endless ways.

.

What do you want with the phone
if you won't answer it.

.

Don't say it doesn't rhyme
if you won't read it—nor break the

line in pieces that goes
and goes and goes.

.

Each moment constitutes reality,
or rather may constitute
reality, or may have *done*
so, or perhaps *will*?

I'd rather sit on my
hands on purpose, and be
an idiot—or just go off somewhere,
like they say, to something else.

.

THE NEWS

Unresponsible
people versus

serious
people. In

New Brunswick
this is a problem.

*

The language
of instruction
for their children . . .

*

The English
speaking people
are not
a numerous group . . .

*

Allentown
Arts Festival
Days . . .

late
film and
video tape
report . . .

        *

NIAGARA MOHAWK

.   .   .

Smell of gum wrappers as of Saturday afternoon at movies
in Maynard, Mass.—

Sudden openness of summer—everything seems to hang
in the air.

      .

I figure

if I eat so much,
I get so fat.

If I don't eat so much
I don't get so fat—

so,
so.

      .

Laugh at the domestic comedy,
the woman falls flat on her face,

the man staggers down the street,
the kid falls down, the dog dies.

Think of the implications,
what you could sell.

.

"It's rare that the city of Buffalo
gets to shape its own destiny . . ."

.

Take advantage of this,
take advantage of what's downtown
and link the two with a
rapid transit system . . .

.   .   .

Where we are there must
be something to place us.
Look around. What do you see
that you can recognize.

.

Anxious about the weather,
folding the door shut, unwrapping
the floor covering and rolling it
forward, at the door.

.

So that's what you do:
ask the same question
and keep answering.

.

Was that right.

.   .   .

The day comes and goes,
the far vistas of the west
are piles of clouds and
an impending storm. I see
it all now—nothing more.

.

Love in a
car takes my
wife away from me.

She is busy. She thinks
in an activity and goes
about her own business.

.

Love one.
Kiss two.

.

In my own ego structure, have to find *place* for shift in
imagination of experience—or else—more probably—
walk as ever, even sentimentally, straight ahead. In age of
hanging gardens variety, now,—all possible, either way—
and times insist on "no problems". That way, so to speak,
there never was.—One wants *one.*

                                        "Love,
                                            Bob"

.   .   .

The first
time is
the first

time. The
second
time think
again.

.

There you
were,
all
the time.

.

I can
not give
it back.

.

Your was there
here in any
way you
were.

.   .   .

MAZATLAN: SEA

The sea flat out,
the light far out,
sky red, the
blobs of dark clouds
seem closer, beyond
the far lateral of
extended sea.

.

Shimmer of reflected
sand tones, the flat
ripples as the water
moves back—an oscil-
lation, endlessly in-
stinct movement—leaves
a ribbing after itself
it then returns to.

.

Bird flicker, light
sharp, flat—the
green hills of the two
islands make a familiar
measure, momently seen.

.

The air is thick
and wet and
comfortably encloses
with the sea's sounds.

.

Sleep—it washes
away.

. . .

Kids walking beach,
minnow pools—
who knows which.

.

Nothing grand—
The scale is neither
big nor small.

.

Want to get the sense of "I" into Zukofsky's "eye"—a
locus of experience, not a presumption of expected value.

.

Here now—
begin!

. . .

B—

Crazy kid-face
skun, in water—
wide hips. The white,
white skin—a big
eared almost feral
toothed woman—
lovely in all particulars.

.

Other way—dark
eyed, the face a
glow of some other
experience, deepens
in the air.

. . .

Agh—man
thinks.

.

Moving away in time,
as they say: *days
later.* Later than this—
what swings in the day's
particulars, one to one.

.

An unexamined hump
at first of no
interest lifting out
of the beach at
last devoured us all.

.

Sell the motherfucker for
several hundred dollars.

.

". . . I ran out of my cabin, both glad and frightened,
shouting, 'A noble earthquake! A noble earthquake!' feel-
ing sure I was going to learn something." [John Muir,
The Yosemite, p. 59.]

.   .   .

The kick
of the foot against . . .

.

Make time
of irritations,
looking for the
recurrence—

waiting, waiting,
on the edge of its
to be there
where it was, waiting.

.

Moving in the mind's
patterns, recognized
because there is where
they happen.

.

Grease
on the hands—

. . .

FOUR

Before I die.
Before I die.
Before I die.
Before I die.

. . .

How that fact of
seeing someone you love away
from you in time will
disappear in time, too.

.

108

Here is all there is,
but *there* seems so
insistently across the way.

.

Heal it, be
patient with
it——be quiet.

.

Across the
table,
years.

.   .   .

HERE

Past time——those
memories opened
places and minds,
things of such reassurance——

now the twist,
and what was a road
turns to a circle
with nothing behind.

.

I didn't know what I could do.
I have never known it
but in doing found it
as best I could.

109

Here I am still,
waiting for that discovery.
What morning, what way now,
will be its token.

.

They all walk by
on the beach,
large, or little,
crippled, on the face
of the earth.

.

The wind holds
my leg like

a warm hand.

. . .

Some nights, a fearful
waking—beside me
you were sleeping,
what your body was

a quiet, apparent
containment. All the world is
this tension, you or me,
seen in that mirror,

patient, pathetic, insured.
I grow bored with lives
of such orders—my own
the least if even yours the most.

.

No one lives in
the life of another—
no one knows.

In the singular
the many cohere,
but not to know it.

Here, here, the body
screaming its orders,
learns of its own.

.

What would you have
of the princess—
large ears, to hear?
Hands with soft fingers?

You will ride away
into the forest, you will
meet her there
but you will know her.

Why not another
not expected, some
lovely presence suddenly
declared?

All in your mind
the body is, and of
the body such
you make her.

.

One, two,
is the rule—

from there to three
simple enough.

Now four
makes the door

back again
to one and one.

     .

My plan is
these little boxes
make sequences . . .

     .

Lift me
from such I
makes such declaration.

     .

Hearing it—*snivelling*—
wanting the reassurance of
another's decision.

There is no one precedes—
look ahead—and behind
you have only where you were.

  . . .

You see the jerked
movement, in the
rigid frame, the
boy—the tense stricken

animal, and behind,
the sea moves and
relaxes. The island sits
in its immovable comfort.

What, in the head, goes wrong—
the circuit suddenly
charged with contraries,
and time only is left.

.

The sun drops. The swimmers
grow black in the silver
glitter. The water slurs
and recurs. The air is soft.

. . .

Could write of fucking—
rather its instant or the slow
longing at times of its approach—

how the young man desires,
how, older, it is never known
but, familiar, comes to be so.

How your breasts, love,
fall in a rhythm also familiar,
neither tired nor so young they

push forward. I hate the metaphors.
I want you. I am still alone,
but want you with me.

. . .

Listless,
the heat rises—
the whole beach

vacant,
sluggish.
The forms shift

before we know,
before we thought
to know it.

The mind
again, the manner
of mind in the

body, the
weather, the waves,
the sun grows lower

in the faded
sky. Washed
out—the afternoon

of another day
with other people,
looking out of other eyes.

Only the
children, the sea,
the slight wind move

with the
same insistent
particularity.

.

I was sleeping
and saw the context

of people, dense
around me, talked
into their forms, almost

strident. There were
bright colours, intense
voices. We were, like
they say, discussing

some point of procedure—
would they go, or
come—and waking,
no one but my wife there,
the room faint, bare.

                    .

"It's strange. It's
all fallen
to grey."

                    .

How much
money is
there now?

Count it
again. There's
enough.

                    .

What changes.
Is the weather
all there is.

            .   .   .

Such strangeness of mind I know
I cannot find there more
than what I know.

I am tired of purposes,
intent that leads itself
back to its own belief. I want

nothing more of such brilliance
but what makes the shadows darker
and that fire grow dimmer.

.

Counting age as form
I feel the mark of one
who has been born and grown
to a little past return.

The body will not go
apart from itself to be
another possibility.
It lives where it finds home.

Thinking to alter all
I looked first to myself,
but have learned the foolishness
that wants an altered form.

Here now I am at best,
or what I think I am
must follow as the rest
and live the best it can.

.

There was no one there.
Rather I thought I saw her,
and named her beauty.

For that time we lived
all in my mind
with what time gives.

The substance of one
is not two. No thought
can ever come to that.

I could fashion another
were I to lose her.
Such is thought.

.

Why the echo of
the old music
haunting all? Why

the lift and fall
of the old rhythms,
and aches and pains.

Why one, why two,
why not go utterly
away from all of it.

.

Last night's dream of a complex of people, almost
suburban it seemed, with plots to uncover like a thriller.
One moment as we walk to some house through the dark,
a man suddenly appears behind us who throws himself at
us, arms reaching out, but falls short and lands, skids,
spread-eagled on the sidewalk. Then later, in another
dream, we are bringing beer somewhere on a sort of truck,
rather the cab of one, nothing back of it, and I am hanging
on the side which I realize is little more than a scaffold-

117

ing—and the wheels nearly brush me in turning. Then, much later, I hear our dog yelp—three times it now seems—so vividly I'm awake and thinking he must be outside the door of this room though he is literally in another country. Reading Yeats: "May we not learn some day to rewrite our histories, when they touch upon these things?"

.   .   .

When he and I,
after drinking and
talking, approached
the goddess or woman

become her, and by my
insistence entered
her, and in the ease
and delight of the

meeting I was given that
sight gave me myself,
this was the mystery
I had come to—all

manner of men, a
throng, and bodies of
women, writhing, and
a great though seemingly

silent sound—and when
I left the room to them,
I felt, as though hearing
laughter, my own heart lighten.

.

What do you do,
what do you say,
what do you think,
what do you know.

IN LONDON   3

That day
in an oak tree—
fall's way
comes here.

.

Interrupt-
ions.

.

The room's spaces make the place
of the two persons' sitting seem
years across. One might accept
the "place" of one moving off as
in films a double image per-
mits that separation to be realized.

.

Fire the
half burnt
log, burning,
lies on.

.

Waked to past now dream
of previous place was about to
get all the confusions at last
resolved when he then woke up.

.

What is the
day of the
year we
sit in with
such fear.

.   .   .

123

We'll die
soon enough,
and be dead—

whence the whole
system
will fade from my head—

"but why the
tort-
ure . . ." as if

another circumstance
were forever
at hand.

.

Thinking of dying
á la Huxley on
acid so that
the beatific smile his
wife reported
was effect possibly
of the splendour of
all *possible* experience?

Or else, possibly,
the brain cells,
the whole organism,
exploding, im-
ploding, upon
itself, a galaxy
of light, energy,
forever more.

.

Die. Dead,
come alive.

.

SIGN

What you know of me—
pale water.
The wind moves

that scattered cloud.
The shimmer of the air,
the sunlight

are perfect
in the mind,
the body.

.

Pacing as with some consequent
expectance, viz—"look out"—
the expected sequence then waited for.

.

Come fly with me—like,
out of your mind is
no simile, no mere
description—what "mere",
mare, mère, mother—
"here then", is what you want.

.

Emily—simile.
What are you
staring at?

.

I wanted to find something
worthy of respect—like
my family, any one one knows.

.

What are you crossing all
those out for. A silence lasting
from then on . . .

.

Those out for.
From then on.

Round and round
all the corners.

.   .   .

Love—
let it

Out,
open up

Very,
very *voraciously*—

Everywhere,
everyone.

.   .   .

BOBBIE'S LAW

"Every one
having the two."

.

Get it any way
you can but first of all
eat it.

.

Time to go
back where you
were going.

.

"Dicky the Stick"—
a stick.

. . .

THE EDGE

Place it,
make the space

of it. Yellow,
that was a time.

He saw the stain of love
was upon the world,

a selvage, a faint
afteredge of colour fading

at the edge of the world,
the edge beyond that edge.

.

You think in the circle
round the whole.

.

Now there is
still something.

. . .

LITTLE TIME—
AND PLACE

You don't say
it is no
answer—you

don't say
it is no
answer.

.

After and after
round and around.

. . .

The so-called poet of love
is not so much silent as absorbed.
He ponders. He sits on
the hill looking over . . .

.

A day late—
your love was
still there.

.

Little bits
of it.

.

They are useful
people.

.

No sense one
should be different.

.   .   .

Dead in the year—
forms make friends.

.   .   .

"Fine China.
A dollar twenty-nine."

.   .   .

In the
mouth—a
hand.

.

Hair is a
long thing

hanging
off.

.

Out the door
the
ass is
a
way.

.

Sitting—
shitting.

.

Fine manners,
weather,
cars and
people.

    .

No air is
in this
room but
the sounds
occupy all
the space.

. . .

Rippling eyelids
with glister of moisture—

Long time no see.

. . .

THE TEACHINGS

of my grandmother
who at over eighty
went west from West Acton,
to see a long lost son named
Archie—by Greyhound, my
other uncle, Hap, got the *Globe*
to photograph her, and us—
came back from Riverside, California,
where Archie was—he'd left
at eighteen—and he'd tried,
she told us, to teach her
religion, "at her age"—"as

much a fool as ever"——and
she never spoke of him again.

. . .

Dreary, heavy
accumulation
of guilts, debts—
all in the head.

.

A wind I can
hear outside shifts
the mind, day, eye's
centre. A kind.

.

KIKI

World in a
plastic octa-
gon from a
most perspica-
cious daughter.

. . .

A WALL
for Tom

Afternoon lengthens like sunlight
also shrinking as the day comes
to its end in the flickering light.

The leaves make it like that,
the wind moves them, the trees
tower so high above the room's space.

I had walked into a wall, not
through but against it, felt my
shoulder hit its literal hardness.

Sunday. Nothing to worship but
myself, my own body and those
related—my wife, my children, my friends—

but outside, light, it grows long,
lenghens. This world of such changes,
nothing stable but in that motion.

Oh spaces. Dance. Make happiness.
Make the simple the changing—
a little ode to much hopefulness.

.

All around
the town
he walked.

.   .   .

The men in my life were
three in number, a
father, uncle, grand-

father—and with that
father an interchangeable
other—the *Man*—whom

to score with, scream at.
The *wind* rises in a
fucking, endless volume.

.   .   .

Neither sadness nor desire
seems the edge: this precipice.

.

Delight dances,
everything works.

.

How wise age is—
How desirous!

.

Love's faint trace . . .

.

The smell of stale air
in this cramped room.
One sits. The shit falls
below the seat into water.

.

You have nor face nor hands
nor eyes nor head either.

. . .

IN LONDON
for Bettina

Homage to Bly & Lorca

———————————————

"I'm going home to Boston
by God"

.

Signs

(red)

EXIT
EXIT
EXIT
EXIT

.

(Cards)

Question—
where do you get a pencil.
Answer.
_____

.

(for Jim Dine)

most common simple
address words everything
in one clear call to me.

.

("Small Dreams")

Scaffolding comes up the side of the building, pipes,
men putting them there. Faces, in, past one block of win-
dows, then as I'm up in the bathroom, they appear there
too.

.

Ted
is ready.
The bell
rings.

.

Small dreams of home.
Small of home dreams.
Dreams of small home.
Home small dreams of.

.

I love you happily
ever after.

.

(Homesick, etc.)

There is a land
far, far away
and I will go there
every day.

.

12.30 (Read as Twelve Thirty)

(Berrigan
Sleeps on)

.

Voices on the phone, over it—wires? Pulsations. Lovely
one of young woman. Very soft and pleasant. Thinking of
Chamberlain and Ultra Violet—"talking the night away".
Fuck MacCluhan—or how the hell you spell it—and/or
teetering fall, the teething ring, "The Mother of Us All"—
for Bob. Call me up. "Don't Bring Me Down . . ."

.

Variance of emotional occasion in English voices—for
myself, American, etc. Therefore awkward at times "to
know where one is". In contrast to Val's Welsh accent—

the congruence with one's own, Massachusetts. Not that
they "sound alike"—but somehow do agree.

.

"London
Postal Area
A-D"

.

Posterior possibilities—
Fuck 'em.

.

"It's 2 hrs. 19 mins. from London
in the train to beautiful country."

.

"EAT ME"
The favourite delicious dates.

.

Girls
Girls
Girls
Girls

2 X 2

.

Some guy now here inside wandering around with ladder
and bucket. Meanwhile the scaffolding being built outside
goes on and on, more secure.

Like German's poem I once translated, something about "when I kissed you, a beam came through the room. When I picked you flowers, they took the whole house away". Sort of an ultimate hard-luck story.

.

Lovely roofs outside.
Some of the best roofs in London.

.

Surrounded
by bad art.

.

I get
a lot
of writing
done—

"You Americans."

.

H— will pirate primary edition of Wms' *Spring and All*, i.e., it's all there. Check for Whitman's *An American Primer*—long time out of print. Wish he'd reprint as Chas apparently suggests Gorki's *Reminiscences of Tolstoi* [now learn it's been in paperback for some years]. Wish I were home at this precise moment—the sun coming in those windows. The sounds of the house, birds too. Wish I were in bed with Bobbie, just waking up.

.

Wish I were an apple seed
and had John what's-his-name
to plant me.

.

Her strict eye,
her lovely voice.

.

Cosi fan tutti.
So machin's alle.

.

Wigmore
dry gin
kid.

.

Wish Joan Baez was here
singing "Tears of Rage" in my ear.

Wish I was Bob Dylan—
he's got a subtle mind.

.

I keep coming—
I keep combing my hair.

.

Peter Grimes
Disraeli Gears

.

That tidy habit of sound
relations—must be in the
very works,* like.

---

* Words work
the author of many pieces

.

138

Wish could snap pix in
mind forever of roofs out
window. Print on endurable paper, etc.

.

With delight he realized
his shirts would last him.

.

I'll get home in 'em.

.

The song of such energy
invites me. The song

of

. . .

There is a space
of trees—

long since, all
there—

. . .

S O B I G

The night's eye
he could say
blandly.

A
word goes
forward—

hands down. She
sleeps beside
him, is

139

elsewhere. The
movie goes on,
the people

hurt each other.
Now say to her,
love is all.

.　　.　　.

Sweet, sad
nostalgia—
walking

by on the
beach a
kid in two

piece bathing
suit of awful
colour, girl

with small
breasts, furtive,
half-terrified

a man who
might have been
screaming, a

woman, more
lush, huge, somewhat
fallen

breasts. Waves
coming in as
the tide

goes out, either York Beach,
Maine,
1937 or else

waking, kicking at
the water, the
sand between my toes.

.

Let me see what you're looking at,
behind you, up close, my head pressed

against you, let me look at what
it is you are seeing, all by yourself.

.

Echoes—what
air trembles to
sound out like
waves one watches.

.   .   .

I don't hate you lately,
nor do I think to
hate you

lately. Nor then nor now—
lately—no
hate—for me,

for you.

.

WAY

The walls constituting our
access to the property—

then the path through it,
the walls of that access.

. . .

Looking for a way
the feet find it.

If mistaken, the
hands were not.

Ears hear. Eyes
see everything.

The mind only
takes its time.

.

Blesséd water, blesséd man . . .
How long to find you,
how long looking at what is inevitable?

. . .

SOUP
   for Mike and Joanne

Trembling
with delight—
mind takes forms

from faces,
finds
happiness

delicious . . .

.

People without their own scene
lean.

.

142

TWO TIMES

Image
docteur

ee-maj
dok-turr

That's a beautiful coat.

.

''Your wish came true
to my surprise.''

.   .   .

I want to fuck you
from two to four

endlessly
the possibility

I want to
fuck you

.

Charmed
by his own reward.

.

A trembling now
throughout.

.

I am here.